▲ BEAUTIFUL WATER GARDENS
Japan is well known for its gardens. Balance your trip to Japan's busy cities with a picnic under the trees.

Japan's past

Japan's history is full of stories of princes, **emperors**, **shoguns** and democratic leaders. Read on to learn how Japan became the great nation it is today.

Ancient history

The first settlers in Japan were the Ainu people. By 10,000 BC, the number of people in Japan had grown quickly. The Jomon period of history began. The Jomon people worshipped spirits they believed were part of nature. Their religion became known as Shinto.

In around AD 300, the nation of Japan was formed under its first emperor. This is known as the Yamato period. The Buddhist religion was introduced in the 6th century. It became the most important religion in Japan after Shinto. By 604, Japan had a rich **culture**. Prince Shotoku Taishi created the first **constitution**. About 100 years later, the city of Nara became Japan's capital. The capital was later moved to Kyoto.

The samurai

At the end of the 1100s, the samurai took control of Japan. The samurai were the Japanese warrior class. They ruled for about 600 years. Then civil war broke out among different groups of samurai. The war went on for more than 100 years.

During the 1600s, a man of the Tokugawa family became Japan's leader, or shogun. A new government began in the city of Edo, which is now called Tokyo.

Contents

Welcome to Japan

Japan is a beautiful country. You may be interested in learning about Japan because you want to visit, or perhaps you are simply curious about the country and its people. In this book you will learn about the exciting history of Japan and look at pictures of places you may not have seen or heard about before. You will read about Japan's amazing sights and learn many interesting facts about this fascinating country.

Pronunciation guide

Ainu	I-nyu
Kyoto	KI-oh-toh
Tokugawa Ieyasu	TOH-khu-gah-wah EE-yah-soo
Hokkaido	HOK-i-doh
Kyushu	KIYU-shoo
Ginza	JIN-zah
Asakusa	AH-sah-KU-sah
Obon	o-BOHN

The Tokugawa **dynasty** had an **isolationist policy** that lasted over 200 years. This meant that Japan had contact only with China and the Netherlands.

The isolationist policy ended when Commodore Matthew Perry of the USA came to Japan in 1854. He persuaded Japanese leaders to allow trade with the USA and European nations.

Japan became more modern and adopted Western systems of government. A new government, again under an emperor, was formally set up in 1889.
An assembly of **representatives** called the Diet was created. The emperor gave money to support schools for the Arts. Japan's traditional Arts grew in importance as a result.

▲ **THE GOLD PAVILION, KYOTO**
A Japanese shogun built this pavilion near the
Imperial Palace in the 1400s. It was burnt down in
1950 and rebuilt. Today it is a religious shrine.

Recent history

Through the early 20th century, Japan's success grew.
Modern factories and businesses sprang up all over the
country. But there was still a wide gap between the poor
and the rich. Some poor farmers started the **Rice Riots**

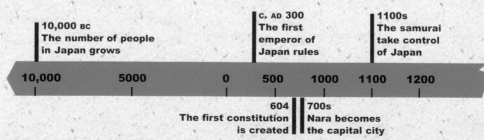

10,000 BC
The number of people
in Japan grows

C. AD 300
The first
emperor of
Japan rules

1100s
The samurai
take control
of Japan

| 10,000 | 5000 | 0 | 500 | 1000 | 1100 | 1200 |

604
The first constitution
is created

700s
Nara becomes
the capital city

in 1918. Then, in 1923, the Great Kanto Earthquake **devastated** the country. Life in Japan became even less **stable**.

Emperor Hirohito began his rule in 1926. His armies invaded China and Korea, and thousands of innocent Chinese and Koreans were killed or imprisoned.

Japan allied with Germany and Italy during World War II. The USA dropped atomic bombs on the cities of Hiroshima and Nagasaki in 1945. Japan surrendered after the devastation caused by the atomic bombs.

Japan today

Japan adopted a new constitution in 1945 and promised to become a peace-seeking **democracy**. In 1956 Japan was invited to join the United Nations, an assembly of representatives from countries around the world. There was one condition: Japan's military could only defend the country and not wage war against other countries.

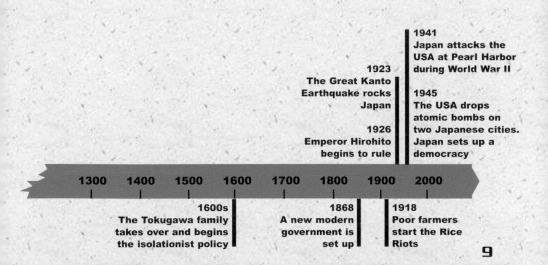

1923
The Great Kanto
Earthquake rocks
Japan

1926
Emperor Hirohito
begins to rule

1941
Japan attacks the
USA at Pearl Harbor
during World War II

1945
The USA drops
atomic bombs on
two Japanese cities.
Japan sets up a
democracy

1300 1400 1500 1600 1700 1800 1900 2000

1600s
The Tokugawa family
takes over and begins
the isolationist policy

1868
A new modern
government is
set up

1918
Poor farmers
start the Rice
Riots

A look at Japan's geography

Four main islands make up Japan. More than 125 million people inhabit this land. Beautiful little towns dot the countryside and mountains. In crowded cities like Tokyo, there are modern, towering buildings, bright lights and nightclubs. There are also lovely parks where people can relax.

Land

Japan is shaped a bit like a seahorse. The four main islands in the country are Hokkaido, Honshu, Shikoku and Kyushu. There are also more than 3900 smaller islands spread across the south. There is a huge difference in **climate** between the north and south of Japan. In the north it is cold and snowy. In the south there are pretty tropical islands and coral reefs.

Mountains cover 80 per cent of Japan. Many are volcanoes, at least 60 of which are still active. Japan's most famous mountain is Mount Fuji, which is also a volcano. Mount Fuji is the country's highest point at 3776 metres tall. The last time Mount Fuji erupted was in 1707.

The mountains are usually too steep for building farms or homes on. Most people live on the **plains** along the coasts of Japan or in the valleys between the steep mountains. Over 80 per cent of Japan's population lives in the low-lying lands.

JAPAN'S SIZE ▶

Japan stretches 2250 km (1400 miles) from north-east to south-west. It measures 320 km (200 miles) wide. It is on average about 500 km (310 miles) off the mainland of Asia. Across the Sea of Japan are Russia, China and Korea.

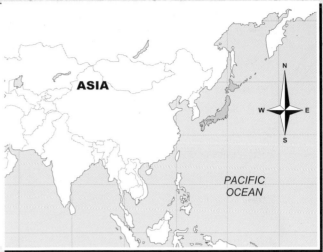

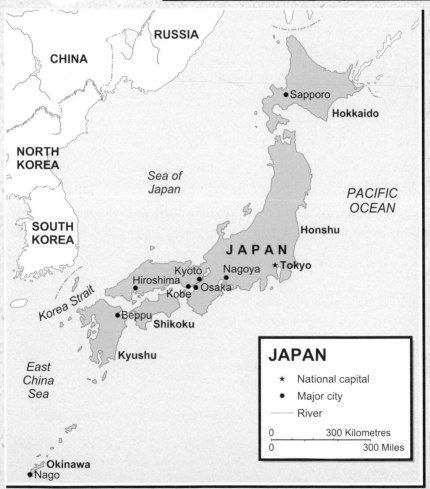

JAPAN

★ National capital
● Major city
— River

0   300 Kilometres
0   300 Miles

Water

Japan is an island nation so it is surrounded by water. The Sea of Japan is in the west. It separates Japan from South Korea, North Korea and Russia. To the east is the vast Pacific Ocean. The USA and Canada are more than 8000 kilometres (5000 miles) to the east across the Pacific Ocean.

Between Japan's mountain ranges lie sparkling rivers and streams. The longest river in Japan is the Shinano. It flows for 367 kilometres (228 miles) from the mountains of central Honshu to the Sea of Japan.

Japan's largest freshwater lake is Lake Biwa. It is south of central Honshu, near Kyoto. Lake Biwa covers over 672 square kilometres (259 square miles).

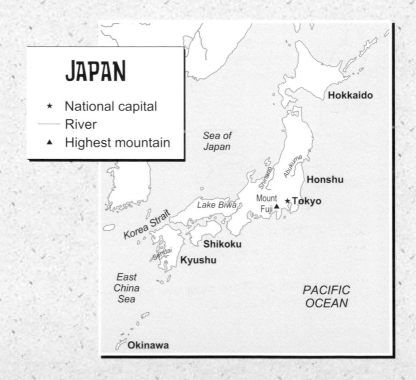

JAPAN

★ National capital
— River
▲ Highest mountain

Sea of Japan

Hokkaido

Shinano

Abukuma

Honshu

Lake Biwa

Mount Fuji ▲

★ Tokyo

Korea Strait

Shikoku

Sendai

Kyushu

East China Sea

PACIFIC OCEAN

Okinawa

MONKEYS ▶

These monkeys are enjoying their bath in the hot water springs of Beppu on the island of Kyushu.

▲ LAKE TOWADA IN AUTUMN

Lake Towada is a great place to visit in the autumn. The leaves on all the trees change colour as the seasons change. From here you will have a perfect view of Mount Hakkoda.

Weather

The weather in Japan is different in the northern, central and southern regions. The most northern region, Hokkaido, is very cold and snow falls often there. Hokkaido's summer is very short and cool. Temperatures rise to a maximum of 23°C.

Okinawa is a small island in the south of Japan. Temperatures there reach around 30°C in summer and in winter it is one of the warmest parts of Japan.

Western and eastern areas of Japan are affected by powerful, seasonal winds called monsoons. Monsoons in the summer come from the Pacific. They make the southern and central areas hot and **humid**. In winter, monsoons from northern Asia bring rain and snow on the western coasts. There is a lot of rain throughout the country because Japan is between two oceans.

The best time to visit Japan is in the spring. The temperatures are warm and the skies are clear. In Japan, spring is the most celebrated season because beautiful cherry trees blossom everywhere. Tourists also enjoy visiting Japan during the autumn when the leaves turn to magical shades of red and gold.

▲ ICE SCULPTURES
The Yuki Matsuri snow festival in Sapporo is legendary.
It is a parade of more than 200 ice sculptures that are lit
up in bright colours.

Tokyo: snapshot of a big city

▲ **BIG CITY, BRIGHT LIGHTS**
One of the world's biggest and busiest cities, Tokyo is modern and exciting. It is crowded, too – the underground trains have guards to squeeze people into the carriages.

Tourists who visit Japan often make the city of Tokyo, Japan's capital, their first stop. It hosts skyscraper buildings that look like scenes from a comic book. Flashy billboards and lights brighten its business and commercial districts. You will be able to find the latest electronics and toys. Old wooden houses are tucked in between new tall buildings. The mix of old and new in Tokyo is breathtaking.

City facts

Over 30 million people live in the city area of Tokyo, making it one of the largest cities in the world. Tokyo was originally a small fishing village called Edo. The city turned into an important trading route because ships would come to the **port** of Yokohama. In the 1400s, a castle was built to guard the trading route. A samurai leader, the shogun Tokugawa Ieyasu, conquered the castle and made the city his base. In 1868, the emperor moved his capital from Kyoto to Tokyo.

The city has dealt with many tragedies. A huge fire in 1657 ruined all the important wooden buildings and temples. In 1923, the Great Kanto Earthquake flattened the port of Yokohama, killing over 100,000 people. During World War II, Tokyo was continually bombed. Most historic buildings were destroyed.

After World War II, Japan rebuilt its capital. Tokyo now has tall office buildings and busy shopping streets. It has museums, teahouses and kabuki theatres. Kabuki is a traditional form of Japanese theatre. It began in the 17th century. There are no women actors in Kabuki theatre, so men dress up and play the female characters. They wear beautiful costumes and often dance and play music. Tokyo is also packed with ancient **shrines** and temples to visit.

The Ginza area in Tokyo is a great place for going window-shopping. It is a modern shopping district where visitors can try out all the latest technological gadgets, buy souvenirs and gifts to take home and try some of the delicious Japanese snacks sold at the restaurants and bakeries. If you can, go on a Sunday or a public holiday when the streets are closed to traffic.

The underground train system in Japan is excellent. It is the fastest and cheapest way to travel around Tokyo. Taxis are expensive and the traffic is heavy in the city, so walking and taking the train are the best and quickest ways to get around.

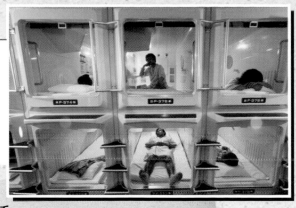

THE WORLD'S SMALLEST HOTEL ROOM? ▶
Many visitors to Tokyo stay in 'capsule hotels' – where they have just enough room to lie down.

TOKYO'S TOP-TEN CHECKLIST

If you are heading to Tokyo, here is a list of the top ten things you should do.

- ☐ Go shopping in the Ginza district.
- ☐ Visit the Senso-ji Temple and old theatres.
- ☐ See the biggest collection of Japanese art in the world at the Tokyo National Museum.
- ☐ Explore the National Science Museum.
- ☐ Watch the Tokyo Giants play baseball in the Tokyo Dome.
- ☐ Look at the animals at Ueno Zoo.
- ☐ Try out the latest video games at the grand Sony Building.
- ☐ Visit the ancient city of Kamakura just outside Tokyo to see the enormous statue of the Great Buddha.
- ☐ Take the underground to explore faraway parts of Tokyo.
- ☐ Go up Tokyo Tower for a beautiful view of the entire city.

Four top sights

To capture the magic of Japan on your visit, here are four places you will not want to miss: Mount Fuji, Peace Memorial Park in the city of Hiroshima and the cities of Nago and Beppu.

Mount Fuji

Mount Fuji has a perfectly shaped snow-topped cone. The mountain is in central Honshu. People can climb Mount Fuji but it is very difficult to reach the top. Most of the mountain is covered with beautiful trees but towards the top it is all black **volcanic rock**. The mountain is open to the public for climbing from 1 July to 27 August each year. Over 400,000 people try to climb it every year and thirty per cent are tourists.

Mount Fuji is considered sacred, or holy. There is a Shinto shrine at the very top of the mountain. The shrine was made in honour of Konohana Sakuya Hime, a divine princess. Shinto **pilgrims** are often seen climbing Mount Fuji during the summer. You will recognize them because they wear traditional white tunics as they climb the mountain.

▲ **THE HIGHEST PEAK IN JAPAN**
Mount Fuji, sacred to the Japanese, is at the heart of Japan.
If you climb to the top, be sure to visit the Shinto shrine there,
which is dedicated to a divine princess.

▲ PAPER CRANES OF PEACE
School children in Japan make thousands of cranes (a type of bird) out of colourful pieces of folded paper. The cranes are placed under this monument at Peace Memorial Park, in memory of the people who died in the nuclear attack that ended World War II.

Peace Memorial Park

Peace Memorial Park is in western Honshu, in the city of Hiroshima. This is where the USA dropped an atomic bomb in 1945, towards the end of World War II.

A number of monuments are in the centre of the city. These include Peace Memorial Museum and Peace Memorial Hall. It is important to visit the park to learn about Japanese history and the effects of war.

In Memorial Park there is a statue which was built to **commemorate** a young girl called Sadako, who died from radiation caused by the atomic bomb. Radiation is invisible energy waves that are dangerous to people. While she was in hospital, Sadako tried to fold a thousand paper cranes in hope of recovering from her illness. Sadly she died after completing only 664. In memory of her and the devastation from World War II, Japanese children leave thousands of paper cranes near the statue every year.

FASCINATING FACT

There is a Peace Flame Monument in Peace Memorial Park that burns all day and all night. The flame will not go out until nuclear weapons are abolished throughout the world. An atomic bomb is a nuclear weapon.

Nago

The cherry blossom festival in the city of Nago is famous around the world. The trees bloom each year at the end of January or beginning of February. Visitors come from all over the world to celebrate this amazing sight. Thousands of trees lining streets and parks are covered with thousands of beautiful dark pink flowers.

Spring arrives early in Nago city, which is in the warmest part of southern Japan. The flowers in Nago are darker than on most cherry trees. In northern Japan, the flowers are white and pale pink.

Nago welcomes the blossoming of the cherry trees by holding an enormous weekend festival with parades and dances. There are feasts, musical performances and games. Colourful lanterns and ornaments are used to decorate the streets for the celebration.

The best place to see the cherry blossoms is at Nago Castle. From its position on a large hill, you can see more than 70,000 cherry blossom trees. The castle also offers a perfect view over Nago harbour and the lovely mountains of Okinawa.

▲ **CHERRY BLOSSOM**
Cherry trees bloom throughout Japan at different times of year. The blossom attracts visitors from all over the world.

▲ 'BLOOD POND'
With its red water and rising mist, you can guess how this spa got its name.

Beppu

The port city of Beppu is known for its hot springs. The Japanese word for these is *onsen*. They are in the southern island of Kyushu. Hot springs are natural streams that heat up underground and bubble up to the surface in small pools. The waters are famous for relaxing and healing the body and over 10 million people visit the area every year.

Visitors to Beppu have a choice of eight different springs and many different **spas** to choose from. Beppu offers several different types of spa. One is the Blood Pond Jigoku (*jigoku* means hell) – its waters are famous for their red glow. The colour comes from minerals in the red mud at the bottom. Another is the Ocean Jigoku, where you can relax in hot, sparkling blue water.

Some spas are expensive but there are many that are affordable. Some spas are outdoors, others are indoors. Whichever spa you try, you are sure to enjoy yourself. Spending a day in a spa in Beppu is the perfect way to relax before going back to the city.

Going to school in Japan

Education is very important in Japan. The country boasts one of the world's highest literacy rates – the percentage of the population that can read and write. Many Japanese students go to school six days a week.

On a typical day, students take classes in history, maths and science. They might also learn the traditional tea ceremony and calligraphy, the art of decorative writing. Japanese writing is called *kanji*. It is very hard to learn and takes years to master. Students must learn thousands of different *kanji* symbols to be able to read and write.

After school, many students take additional classes called *juku* which strengthen and develop their numerical, verbal and written skills. Every student must attend *juku* classes to prepare for college entrance exams. Japan has one of the most difficult tests to pass in order to get into good colleges. Students need to go to good colleges to get the best jobs.

▲ LUNCH BREAK
These girls are making the most of their midday break.

Japanese sports

The Japanese enjoy a variety of sports. Baseball is a very popular game. You can see baseball played in major cities throughout the country. Some Japanese baseball players also play in major league baseball in the USA.

Sumo wrestling is Japan's national sport. Sumo Stadium in Tokyo is the most famous stadium for sumo wrestling.

Martial arts in Japan include karate, kendo, aikido and judo. The roots of these skills come from the Chinese. Buddhists in ancient times created martial arts to defend themselves against attacks from bandits.

SUMO WRESTLING ▶
In this sport, very large men try to knock each other out of a ring. This requires great skill and enormous strength.

From farming to factories

Japan's economy now ranks as one of the strongest in the world. During the 1950s and the 1960s, Japan developed industries of all kinds, including car manufacture. By the 1980s, business was booming. Many people worked in car and electronics companies.

Japan's success lies in manufacturing. Japan **imports** fuel and raw materials from other countries. Raw materials like steel are turned into finished products, including cars, ships and consumer goods like electronics. Japan **exports** these products for sale all over the world.

Large corporations play a major role in the Japanese economy. People work hard to keep their corporations strong. They are very loyal to their employers. In turn, corporations are committed to their employees' success. They often provide housing and health care for their workers.

Farming is very important in Japan, even though only about 12 per cent of Japan is farmland and only 5 per cent of the population are farmers. In Japan there is not much land that is flat enough for farming, so crops are very expensive to produce. Rice is the most important crop in Japan. Farmers also grow tobacco, tea, wheat, vegetables and fruits. Fishing is also important. The Japanese have one of the world's largest fishing fleets.

▲ RICE FARMING
Most Japanese people eat rice at every meal. Farmers grow rice in wet fields called rice paddies.

◀ HIGH-TECH
Men and women in business suits rush back and forth in Tokyo's busy stock exchange district. You will see them talking on mobile phones, carrying laptop computers or using other high-tech devices – many made in Japan.

The Japanese government

Japan's government is a democracy. The prime minister is the chief leader of the country. The Diet, or Kokkai, represents the Japanese people. The Diet is made up of 480 members of the Shugiin (House of Representatives) and 247 members of Sangiin (House of Counsellors). The Shugiin are elected for terms of four years, the Sangiin for three or six years. The Diet elects and advises the prime minister.

The emperor of Japan remains the **figurehead** of the nation. After World War II, the emperor was stripped of any real power. US lawyers designed Japan's current government. They modelled it on the system of government in the USA.

Every citizen aged twenty or over is able to vote in Japan and Japanese people are deeply honoured to have this right. There is a special day of celebration for people who have become old enough to vote.

JAPAN'S NATIONAL FLAG

The Japanese flag was adopted in 1870. It is called Hinomaru, which means 'circle of the sun'. The red circle on the white background stands for the sun. This emblem has been meaningful to the Japanese for centuries.

Religions of Japan

Almost 84 per cent of Japanese people practise Shinto and Buddhism. Shinto is the most important and ancient religion in Japan. People who follow Shinto cleanse themselves by performing simple rituals. These rituals, or religious acts, can include offering a coin to the spirit of a shrine or celebrating special occasions with special foods, drinks, dances and prayers.

Buddhism is also popular in Japan. Many Japanese practise both Shinto and Buddhism. There are two branches of Buddhism – Zen and True Pure Land. Zen Buddhism teaches the use of meditation and mindfulness to find inner peace. True Pure Land teaches that people can be saved through prayer.

Some people in Japan follow Christianity. Christians follow the teachings of Jesus as written in the New Testament of the Bible. Even though most Japanese people do not practise Christianity, many still celebrate Christmas or have their weddings in churches.

SACRED SHRINES ▶
Sacred shrines come in many shapes and sizes. They are found all over Japan. They offer a quiet place for people to come and pray or worship.

Japanese food

The Japanese population is known for good health and many Japanese people live to be 100 years old. Scientists have studied the diets of Japanese people to find out how they stay so healthy.

Rice is usually served at every meal, even for breakfast. A typical Japanese meal consists of a combination of rice, noodles, seaweed, miso soup (a salty soup often served with tofu, a soya bean product) and pickled vegetables. Also included is a boiled, fried or steamed serving of meat, fish or vegetables.

Noodles – thick and thin, cold and hot – are a delicious treat. At a noodle bar, you will see the Japanese eat their bowls of noodles quickly and very loudly. In Japan, slurping your noodles shows the chef that they are tasty.

If you go to a restaurant or eat with a Japanese family, you will notice how beautifully they arrange the dishes, chopsticks and food during a meal. Make sure you practise using chopsticks. People in Japan use these pairs of thin sticks instead of knives and forks.

◀ SUSHI
Sushi is popular in Japan. It is made from vegetables or raw fish and rice wrapped in seaweed.

Japan's recipe

CHICKEN TERIYAKI

INGREDIENTS:
2 chicken breasts
6 tbsp soy sauce
2 tbsp sugar
2 tbsp vegetable oil

WARNING:
Never cook or bake by yourself. Always ask an adult to help you in the kitchen.

DIRECTIONS:
Cut the two chicken breasts into small pieces. Mix the soy sauce and sugar in a bowl. Soak the pieces of chicken in the bowl with the sauce for 30 minutes or longer. (The longer you leave the chicken in the sauce, the tastier it gets.) Afterwards, heat a frying pan over medium heat and pour in the vegetable oil. Be careful of the oil splashing. Turn the heat from medium to low. Put the pieces of chicken from the bowl into the pan. Move them around in the pan to cook on all sides. Turn off the heat and pour in the sauce from the bowl. Heat the pan again and simmer on low heat until the sauce becomes thick. Serve with rice and vegetables.

Up close: kendo

Kendo is a form of martial art. It has become very popular all around the world. Girls, boys, men and women practise kendo in schools and universities across Japan. The sport requires great mental and physical skills. Students of kendo are called kendoka.

The way of the sword

Kendo means 'the way of the sword' in Japanese. People wear protective armour and fight with bamboo sticks. The bamboo sticks, called *shinai*, are about 1.2 metres long. They are made of four thin bamboo sticks bound together to form a round tube. In medieval Japan, samurai would fight with real swords instead of sticks.

What do you wear?

Kendoka wear equipment to protect areas that the opponent is targeting. Each player wears *bogu* that covers and protects the head, wrists and abdomen. The gear includes a face mask, breastplate, gloves and a thick cloth shield for the stomach and hips. Kendoka wear a *hakama* (a wide, split skirt) under their protective clothes.

▲ **SAFETY FIRST**
Kendo students put on safety equipment to prepare for their sport. Kendo is similar to sword fighting and can be very dangerous.

The rules of kendo

Two people play against each other in kendo. Kendoka try to strike their opponent with the top third of their stick. They must shout out the place where they are trying to strike their opponent. The first player to score two points wins.

There are four places the kendoka can aim for on the body. The first, *men*, is a blow to the centre of the head. *Tsuki*, the second, is a straight thrust to the throat. The third is *migi-do*, a strike to the right side of the abdomen. The fourth is *hidari-do*, a strike to the left side of the abdomen.

Where do you learn kendo?

There are kendo schools all over the world. The schools are called *dojos*. There are different classes for younger and older people. There are also classes for each skill level. If you are interested in learning kendo, find your local dojo on the Internet or in the telephone directory.

Holidays

The people of Japan celebrate many national and religious holidays. New Year's Day is one of the most important. The holiday lasts from New Year's Eve until 3 January. People clean their houses from top to bottom, inside and out. They eat a special pounded rice treat called mochi. They put decorations made of tree branches outside their houses. Most Japanese visit Shinto shrines or Buddhist temples to pray for good health and happiness for the year.

Obon is another important celebration. This festival takes place in the middle of August (or July, depending on the lunar calendar). During the festival, people gather at temples. They celebrate by dressing up in kimonos, dancing, singing and eating special foods with family and friends. Obon is a Buddhist tradition, but everyone celebrates the holiday. People also pay their respects to their dead ancestors during the Obon festival.

◀ **TRADITIONAL DRESS**
Japanese women still wear kimonos for special occasions. A kimono is a traditional kind of dress or robe that is tied with a wide sash called an obi.

Learning the language

English	Japanese	How to say it
Hello	Konichiwa	KON-NEE-CHEE-WA
Goodbye	Sayonara	SA-YO-NA-RA
Thank you!	Domo arigato	DO-MO A-RI-GA-TO
How much?	Ikura desuka...	EE-KU-RA DE-SU-KA
Where is it?	Doko desuka	DO-KO DE-SU-KA

Quick facts

Japan

Capital
Tokyo

Borders
Sea of Okhost (N)
Pacific Ocean (E)
Sea of Japan (W)
China Sea (SW)

Area
377,835 sq km
(145,882 sq miles)

Population
126,974,628

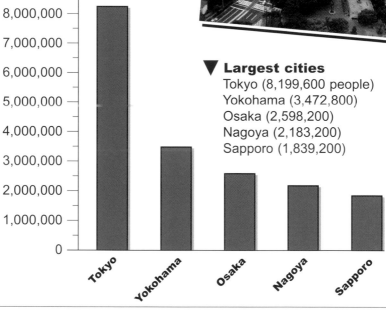

▼ **Largest cities**
Tokyo (8,199,600 people)
Yokohama (3,472,800)
Osaka (2,598,200)
Nagoya (2,183,200)
Sapporo (1,839,200)

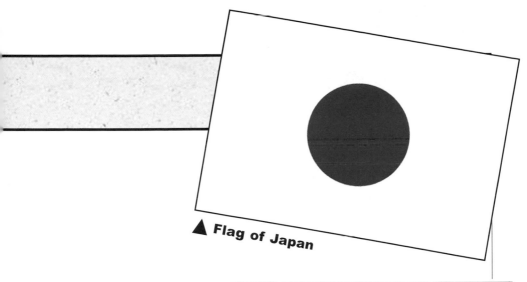

▲ **Flag of Japan**

Longest river
Shinano
367 km (228 miles) long

Coastline ▶
29,751 km
(18,487 miles)

Literacy rate
99% of all Japanese people
can read

Major industries
Cars, electronic products,
engineering, machinery

Chief crops
Rice, sugar beet, vegetables

Natural resources
Mineral resources, fish

◀ **Monetary unit**
Yen

People to know

◀ Emperor Hirohito

Hirohito became emperor in 1926. After World War II, Emperor Hirohito became a marine biologist and a popular symbolic leader.

Seiko Matsuda ▶

Seiko Matsuda is known as the Madonna of Japan. The famous pop singer became popular in the 1980s when she had 24 number-one hits in a row. She continues to attract fans from all over the world. Her good looks, winning smile and melodic voice have won the hearts of young Japanese girls as well as the rest of the nation.

◀ Akira Kurosawa

Akira Kurosawa is one of the most famous film directors in the world. He created several well-known films set in medieval Japan. Kurosawa won the Venice Film Festival's grand prize in 1951. His films put Japanese cinema on the world map.

Do you want to know more about Japan? Have a look at the books below.

Nations of the World: Japan, Jen Green
    (Raintree, 2003)
Explore Japan in detail, from its ancient traditions to its modern high-tech goods. Read more about the history, culture and economy of this important nation.

Next Stop: Japan Fred Martin
    (Heinemann Library, 2001)
Go on a full tour of Japan and learn about its past and present. Discover amazing things about its weather, land and animals. Find out what it is really like to live there.

Turning Points in History: Hiroshima The Shadow of the Bomb, Richard Tames
    (Heinemann Library, 1998)
Learn about the key events and the cause and effect of the dropping of the atomic bomb on Hiroshima. Find out what made this event an important turning point in history.

World of Recipes: Japan, Julie McCulloch
    (Heinemann Library, 2001)
Discover how to make your favourite Japanese recipes and some more unusual ones too.

Glossary

atomic bomb type of nuclear weapon

climate typical weather pattern of a place

commemorate honour or remember a special person or event

constitution written laws that state the rights of the people and how the government will operate

culture way of life of a society or civilization

democracy government in which the leaders are elected by the people

devastated ruined by a catastrophe such as an earthquake

dynasty rulers of a country who are related to each other, such as fathers and sons

emperor ruler of an empire (a very large area, sometimes made up of many countries)

export send a product to another country for sale

figurehead person who holds an important position or office but has no real power

fresh water water that does not contain salt, such as in lakes and natural springs

humid weather that is damp and hot

import buy a product from another country

isolationist policy country's plan to stay separate from other countries by not trading with them or allowing foreign visitors

pilgrim person who goes on a journey to a holy place

plains flat, large areas of land

port place where boats can safely dock to load and unload cargo

representative person who is chosen to speak or act for a group

Rice Riots angry groups of poor people who acted against the government in 1918 in order to demand more food

Samurai (SAM-uh-RIE) warrior class that ruled Japan from the 13th century for eight centuries

Shogun (SHOH-guhn) hereditary leader of the Japanese army who ruled the country until the revolution in 1867

shrine sacred place where holy objects are kept

spa holiday resort built next to natural hot springs

stable unchanging

trade buying and selling of goods

volcanic rock rock formed from molten lava

Index